CELINE DION

LET'S TALK ABOUT LOVE

International Consultant: Ben Kaye

Management: Rene Angelil
FEELING PRODUCTIONS INC.
In Montreal:
2540 Boul. Daniel-Johnson, #755
Laval, Quebec
CANADA H7T 2S3

In Toronto:
1131A Leslie Street, Suite 555
Toronto, Ontario
CANADA M3C 3L8
Management Contact: Dave Platel
Business Affairs: Paul Farberman

Celine Dion International Fan Club
P.O. Box 551
Don Mills, Ontario
CANADA M3C 2T6

Project Manager: Carol Cuellar
Art Layout: Nancy Rehm
Production Coordinator: Zoby Perez
Album Art © 1997 Sony Music Entertainment (Canada) Inc.
Photography: Michael Thompson

Inside photos: Luciano Pavarotti and
The Bee Gees - Dimo Safari;
Sir George Martin and Carole King - George Bodnar

contents

Editor's Note:
Warner Bros. Publications and I would like to personally
thank Ben Kaye for his contribution and faith in working with
our production staff to create this songbook.

It is my personal pleasure to have experienced working with
such professionalism.

Carol Cuellar

Dearest Barbra,
Having the privilege of singing with you is certainly
my wildest dream come true. Since I was a child you've always
been someone that I've looked up to as a
model of perfection.
Your incredibly unique voice has
touched me in ways that
I cannot describe
and I'm deeply honoured
that you've given me the
chance to weave
my voice with yours.
I hope and wish that
these special moments
we've spent together will
develop into
a lifelong friendship.

Caro Luciano,
You are the grandest tenor
in the world and
I have been secretly hoping
to sing a love song
with you for a long time.
I have the greatest respect for classical music and I consider it
a rare privilege to have my name next to yours on this album.
P.S. René and I love your cooking...
let's do this more often!

Dear Carole,
   Receiving a song
from you was a great
gift and having
   the pleasure of
singing with you is
   a great thrill.
Tapestry has always been a favourite album
   in our family as well as so many incredible songs
you've written - we grew up with your music,
   and look at us now!

Dear George,
I am a great
fan of the
Beatles and I
   heard a lot about your talent long before I had
   the chance to work under your direction.
You are truly a master at your craft and a total gentleman
   in life. Working with you, the pleasure
      was all mine. You have all my
   love and gratitude, Sir George.

Bee Gees of my heart,
   I fell in love with "Immortality" from the very first time I was
presented with the song. You've written so many beautiful songs
   for the world and I've been singing along with you for years.
      To have this wonderful opportunity to record with you,
and to experience how much fun you are to be with is
   an everlasting souvenir that I will always cherish.

René mon amour,
Through the wind
  I can feel your strength,
through the rain
  I can see your tears,
through the storm
  I can feel your gentleness,
through your emotion
  I can feel my music.
  L.V. Je t'aime

Céline
xoxo...

Dear Mrs. Angelil...
  you've been a very special
part of my life, and I know that
you're still watching over us.

To Karine... I'm with you
  today, more than ever.

Celine supports the
  Cystic Fibrosis Foundation.

MY HEART WILL GO ON
(Love Theme from 'TITANIC')

Words by
JAMES HORNER

Music by
WILL JENNINGS

Verse 1:

1. Ev - 'ry night in my dreams, I see you, I feel____ you.

That Is how I know you go____ on.

THE REASON

Words and Music by
CAROLE KING, MARK HUDSON,
and GREG WELLS

Additional lyrics:

Verse 3:
I'm not giving it up
No more running around spinning my wheel
You came running out of my dream and made it real
I know what I feel, it's you,
It's all because of you.
(To Chorus:)

IMMORTALITY

Words and Music by
BARRY GIBB, ROBIN GIBB
and MAURICE GIBB

TREAT HER LIKE A LADY

Words and Music by
ANDY MARVEL, BILLY MANN
and DIANA KING

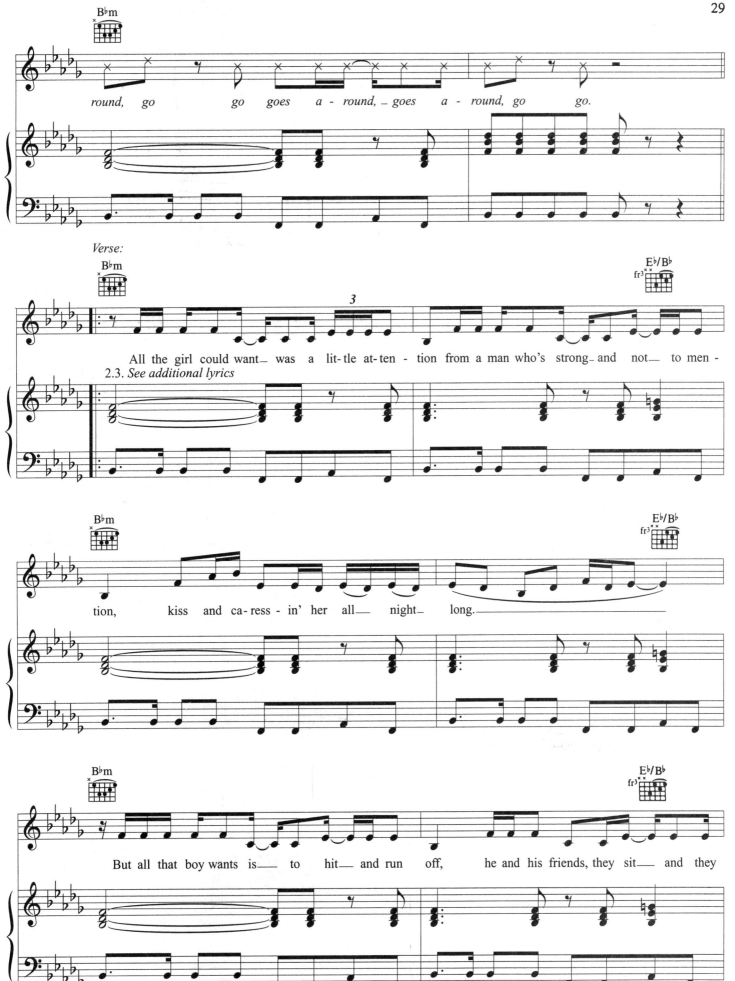

round, go   go goes a - round, — goes a - round, go   go.

Verse:

All the girl could want— was a lit-tle at-ten - tion from a man who's strong— and not— to men -
2.3. *See additional lyrics*

tion,   kiss and ca-ress - in' her all— night— long.—

But all that boy wants is— to hit— and run   off,   he and his friends, they sit— and they

⊕ Coda

la-dy. Treat her like a la - dy, You'll make a

good girl cra-zy if___ you don't treat her like__ a la-dy. Treat her like__ a la-dy,

treat her like__ a la-dy, treat her like__ a la-dy, treat her like__ a la-dy,

Verse 2:

She stopped going to church, she don't wanna go to school
She left with anger when he took her for a fool
Even though her friends tell her to just keep cool.
Didn't tell her from the start just what he had planned
Right in her face with another woman
Now she's in jail for attacking her man.
You're gonna get what's comin' to you,
For all the bad bad things you do
To your lady. . .
(To Chorus:)

Verse 3:

Tell it to her straight, she can take the truth
Don't lead her on and on and leave her confused
Anyone would rather be alone than be used.
Don't sit and think you'll hurt her feelings
She only wants to know just what the deal is
Next time beware of whose heart you're breaking.
You're gonna get what's comin' to you,
For all the bad bad things you do
To your lady. . .
(To Chorus:)

WHY OH WHY

Words and Music by
MARTI SHARRON and DANNY SEMBELLO

Repeat ad lib. to fade

Verse 2:
How can you tell me it was nothing
'Cause you took away everything I dreamed in.
Just a night and I held you so tight
When you know you were sleeping in my bed.
I tried to swallow my pride
But I felt my heart start to tremble inside
Wish I didn't know 'cause I can't let you go.
(To Chorus 2:)

Chorus 2:
Tell me why, why when I looked in your eyes
I felt my heart start to cry
Why oh why
When I saw you with the other girl
Why oh why, why when I looked in your eyes
'Cause I felt the trust start to die
Why oh why
When I still love you
It's so hard to say goodbye.

Verse 3:
(Instrumental 8 bars)

Should I quietly leave through the door
Or maybe pretend the way things were once before
When I met you, I'll never forget you.
(To Chorus:)

LOVE IS ON THE WAY

Words and Music by
PETER ZIZZO, DENISE RICH
and TINA SHAFER

Wak-ing up a-lone in a room that still re-minds me,— my heart has got to learn to for-

2. *See additional lyrics*

get. Start-ing on my own, with ev-'ry breath I'm get-ting strong-er,

find me a - gain.

Love is al-ways on the

way on wings of an - gels, I know it's true, I feel it

Verse 2:
I am not afraid
Of the mystery of tomorrow
I have found the faith within.
There's a promise I have made
There's a dream I'm gonna follow
There's another chance to begin.
And it's coming as sure as the heavens
I can feel it right here in my heart.
(To Chorus:)

TELL HIM

Words and Music by
LINDA THOMPSON, DAVID FOSTER
and WALTER AFANASIEFF

Verse 2:
(Barbra:)
Touch him with the gentleness you feel inside. *(C: I feel it.)*
Your love can't be denied.
The truth will set you free.
You'll have what's meant to be.
All in time, you'll see.
(Celine:)
I love him, *(B: Then show him.)*
Of that much I can be sure. *(B: Hold him close to you.)*
I don't think I could endure
If I let him walk away
When I have so much to say.
(To Chorus:)

WHERE IS THE LOVE

Words and Music by
COREY HART

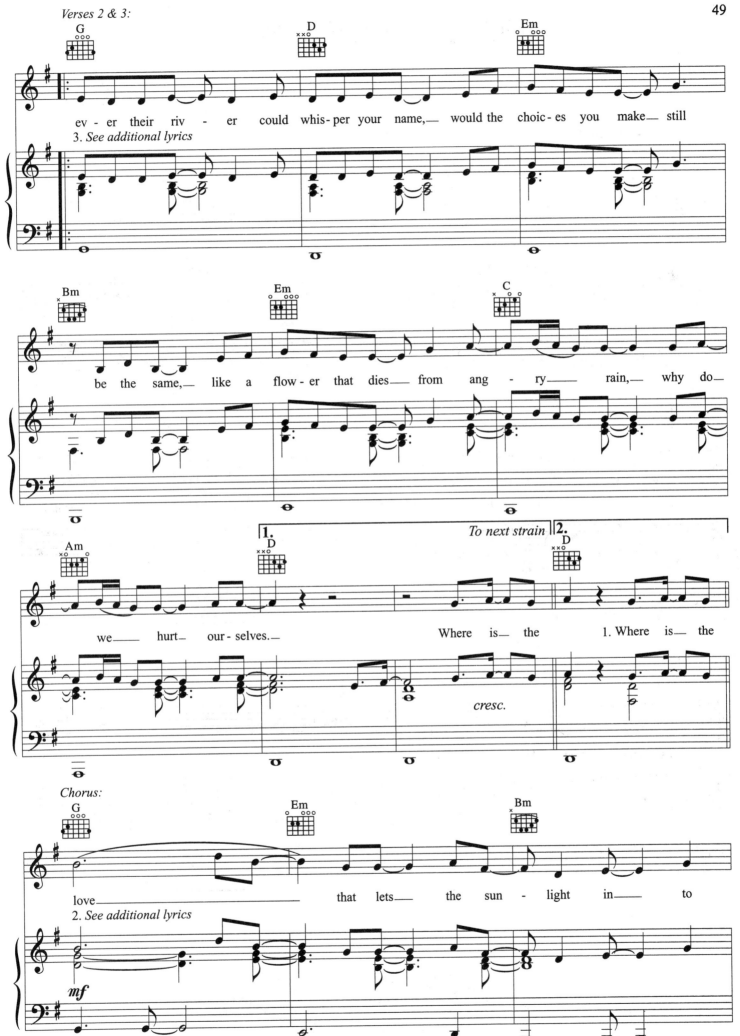

Verse 3:
If ever a boy stood on the moon
Carrying all of his treasures from the stars
To a rainbow which leads to where we are
Together we chase the sun.
(To Chorus 2:)

Chorus 2:
Where is the love
That lifts my brother's voice to the stars?
A love that answers a mothers cry?
Life begins with love.

So spread your wings and fly
Guide your spirit safe and sheltered
A thousand dreams that we can still believe.

Chorus 3 (D.S. 𝄋)

A boy stood on the moon
The ancient souls can still discover
A thousand dreams that we can still believe.

WHEN I NEED YOU

Words by
CAROLE BAYER SAGER

Music by
ALBERT HAMMOND

all that I so want to give you, it's on-ly a heart-beat a - way.___ When I

need love, I hold out my hands and I touch love, I nev-er knew there was so

much love, keep-ing me warm night and day.___

Miles and miles of emp-ty space in be - tween us,

It's not ea - sy when the road is your dri - ver,

a

US

Words and Music by
BILLY PACE

Verse 2:
Once we were one mind
Drifting in one time
And ever true
We were friends
But something is gone from
My picture of this life.
If we could only see
Like we did before
We became imprisoned
Can I reopen the door?
(To Chorus:)

Verse 3:
(Instrumental 6 bars)

If we could only see
Like we did before
We became imprisoned
Can I reopen the door?
(To Chorus:)

MILES TO GO
(Before I Sleep)

Words and Music by
COREY HART

1. I would walk to the edge of the u-ni-verse for you,___ paint you a crim-son sun-set o-ver
2. *See additional lyrics*

shel-ter-ing___ skies.___ I could learn all the world di - a-lects for you,___

whis-per son-nets in your ear, dis-cov-er-ing— truth.—

I could nev-er wor-ship pa-

3. See additional lyrics

- gan gods— a-round me,— I will on-ly fol-low the path— that leads me to you ba-by, al-ways.

Chorus:

Ev-'ry step I take— for— you— I— will al-ways de-fend,—

nev-er pre-tend.— That ev-'ry breath I take— for— love,— I— could

Verse 2:
I would carry the Rock of Gibraltar just for you
Lifted like a pebble from the beach to the skies
I could build you a bridge that spans the ocean wide
But the greatest gift I give you would be to stand by your side.
Some can criticise and sit in judgement of us babe,
But they can't take away the love that lives inside us always.
(To Chorus:)

Verse 3: (D.S. 𝄋.)
I won't run from the changing signs along the highway
Let the rivers flow to the highest ground created.
(To Chorus:)

JUST A LITTLE BIT OF LOVE

Words and Music by
MARIA CHRISTENSEN, ARNIE ROMAN
and ARTIE JACOBSEN

free your soul.

D.%. al Coda

Play 4 times

⊕ Coda

Just a lit - tle bit of

Verse 2:
I found the truth, I found the way
I'm standing in the light of day
I got the power.
I'm not worried any longer
No, I'm only getting stronger by the hour.
You can move a mountain
Or calm the stormy sea,
Baby oh let me see.
There's no doubt about it
I truly do believe, oh baby.
(To Chorus:)

I HATE YOU THEN I LOVE YOU

Words and Music by
TONY RENIS, MANUEL DE FALLA, ALBERTO TESTA,
FABIO TESTA and NORMAN NEWELL

LET'S TALK ABOUT LOVE

Words and Music by
BRYAN ADAMS, JEAN-JACQUES GOLDMAN
and ELLIOT KENNEDY

gen-tle as a fall-ing leaf— on an-y au-tumn morn.— Let's talk a-bout— love, let's talk a-bout—

us,———— let's talk a-bout— life, let's talk a-bout trust.—— Let's talk a-bout—

love, let's talk a-bout— us, let's talk a-bout life, let's talk a-bout—
(It's all we're needing) (It's the air we're breathing) (I wanna know you)

trust.
(And I wanna show you)

Ev - 'ry - where— I go, all the plac - es that I've been,_____ ev - 'ry

smile's a new— ho - ri - zon, on a land I've— nev - er seen.— There are

peo - ple a - round the world,— dif - f'rent fac - es, dif - f'rent names,— but

there's one true e - mo - tion, that re - minds me we're the same.— Let's talk a - bout—

Verse 2:
From the laughter of a child
To the tears of a grown man
There's a thread that runs right through us
And helps us understand.
As subtle as a breeze
That fans a flicker to a flame
From the very first sweet melody
To the very last refrain.

TO LOVE YOU MORE

Words and Music by
DAVID FOSTER and JUNIOR MILES

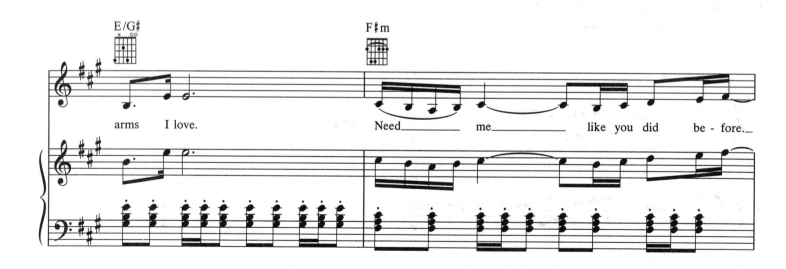

the one___ to___ love___ you___ more.___

Oh.___